Migration

Monica Hughes

www.heinemann.co.uk/library
Visit our website to find out more information about **Heinemann Library** books.

To order:
☎ Phone 44 (0) 1865 888066
▤ Send a fax to 44 (0) 1865 314091
▱ Visit the Heinemann Bookshop at www.heinemann.co.uk/library to browse our
catalogue and order online.

First published in Great Britain by Heinemann Library, Halley Court, Jordan Hill, Oxford OX2 8EJ, part of Harcourt Education. Heinemann is a registered trademark of Harcourt Education Ltd.

Editorial: Jilly Attwood, Kate Bellamy
Design: Jo Hinton-Malivoire
Picture research: Ginny Stroud-Lewis, Ruth Blair
Production: Séverine Ribierre

Originated by Ambassador Litho Ltd
Printed and bound in China by South China Printing Company

ISBN 0 431 11394 7
08 07 06 05 04
10 9 8 7 6 5 4 3 2 1

British Library Cataloguing in Publication Data
Hughes, Monica
Migration - (Nature's Patterns)
591.5'68
A full catalogue record for this book is available from the British Library.

Acknowledgements
The Publishers would like to thank the following for permission to reproduce photographs: Alamy p. **8** (Natural Visions); FLPA pp. **16**, **17** (Minden Pictures); Getty Images/Photodisk pp. **9**, **14**, **22**; Heather Angel pp. **18**, **19**, **20**, **28** (Natural Visions); Ian Montgomery pp. **24**, **25**; NHPA pp. **26**, **27**; NHPA pp. **13** (Paul Hermansen), **29** (Jean Louise Le Moigne); Nature Photo Library pp. **5**, **10**, **11**, **12**, **15**, **23**; Oxford Scientific Films p. **6** (Ian West), **21** (Howard Hall); Science Photo Library pp. **4**, **7**.

Cover photography of Greylag geese on the Isle of Lewis, Scotland, is reproduced with permission of Nature Photo Library.

Our thanks to David Lewin for his assistance in the preparation of this book.

Every effort has been made to contact copyright holders of any material reproduced in this book. Any omissions will be rectified in subsequent printings if notice is given to the Publishers.

The paper used to print this book comes from sustainable resources.

Contents

Nature's patterns   4

Migration   6

Reindeer   8

Wildebeest   10

Lemmings   12

Green sea turtles   14

Grey whales   16

Salmon   18

Spiny lobsters   20

Monarch butterflies   22

Blue-winged parrots   24

Swallows   26

Arctic terns   28

Migration map   30

Glossary   31

More books to read   31

Index   32

Words appearing in the text in bold, **like this**, are explained in the Glossary.

 Find out more about Nature's Patterns at www.heinemannexplore.co.uk

Nature's patterns

Nature is always changing. Many of the changes that happen follow a **pattern**. This means that they happen over and over again.

The American bat travels to warmer places for the winter.

Storks spend the summer in Europe and the winter in South Africa.

Some patterns have a clear beginning and end. Animal journeys, or **migration**, have a pattern. Each has a different pattern and most have a clear beginning and an end.

5

Migration

Many animals make a special journey. They move from their home to live somewhere else. They stay there until it is time to go back home.

Frogs migrate when it is time to mate and lay their eggs.

Snow geese migrate in large flocks and fly in a 'V'-shaped group.

This movement is called **migration**. There are different migration **patterns**. Some animals migrate every year. Others migrate only when they are adults.

Reindeer

Reindeer **migrate** every autumn. They move from the Arctic Circle because the weather gets too cold. The snow makes it hard to find food.

Reindeer eat grass, twigs and moss. The snow stops them finding this food.

The reindeer travel south where it is warmer and there is more food. After winter is over, they go back to the Arctic Circle.

There is plenty of grass for the reindeer to eat here.

Wildebeest

Wildebeest live in Africa. In the dry **season** there is very little rain and the grass has either dried up or been eaten. So, the wildebeest **migrate**.

In the dry season there will not be enough water left in this pool for the wildebeest to drink.

The huge herds of wildebeest often have to swim across rivers on their long journey.

The wildebeest move from place to place in search of water and fresh grass. When the rains come they go back home.

Lemmings

Lemmings live together on mountain **pastures**. Their **migration** follows an unusual **pattern**. It only happens every few years.

Lemmings do not migrate when winter comes, they hide in underground burrows.

A female may have as many as ten young each year and this can lead to overcrowding.

Some years there is lots of food so the lemmings **breed** well. Then there are too many lemmings. So, lots of them migrate, looking for new pastures.

Green sea turtles

Green sea turtles spend most of their lives at sea. Every two or three years they **migrate** to warmer waters near land to **breed**.

Only adult green sea turtles migrate.

After the young turtles **hatch** they head straight for the sea.

Female green sea turtles dig deep holes on the beach. They lay lots of eggs in the sand. Then they go back to where they usually live.

Grey whales

Grey whales spend the summer in the Arctic Ocean where they eat lots of food to build up their **blubber**. They **migrate** when winter comes.

Grey whales migrate from north to south.

The whales **breed** and **rear** their **young** in the sea near California and Mexico. When winter is over they all go back to the Arctic Ocean.

The adults live off their blubber. The mothers feed their babies on milk.

Salmon

Adult salmon live in the sea. They **migrate** to **breed** and lay eggs. They travel back to the same stream or river where they **hatched**.

Adult salmon can remember the smell of the river where they hatched.

Female salmon lay their eggs in the autumn.

On their migration journey salmon may swim up rivers and leap up waterfalls. Their **young** will do the same journey when they are adults.

Spiny lobsters

Spiny lobsters live alone in the sea. Each autumn they get together to **migrate** to deeper water. They line up, one in front of the other.

A spiny lobster will attack others if they come near.

Spiny lobsters move with each lobster holding on to the one in front. When spring comes they go back to living alone.

Spiny lobsters migrate to warmer water to stay away from storms and rough waves.

Monarch butterflies

Every year monarch butterflies make a big journey. In the winter they travel from Canada and northern USA to California and Mexico, where it is warm.

The monarch butterfly lives alone in the summer.

The butterflies use the same trees each year as resting places when they fly south.

Monarch butterflies **migrate** before the cold winter weather comes. In huge groups, they fly south to the warmer weather. After winter, they fly back north to **breed**.

23

Blue-winged parrots

Most parrots live all year in their own part of a rainforest. Blue-winged parrots are unusual because they **migrate**. They spend winter in south-east Australia.

The blue-winged parrot gets its name from the patch of blue on its wing.

Blue-winged parrots live in the Australian rainforest in the winter.

Blue-winged parrots fly a long distance from Australia to Tasmania. This is where they spend summer. They **breed** and **rear** their **young** there before flying back.

25

Swallows

Swallows **migrate** each year as the **seasons** change. Every spring they come to live in the UK. They build nests, lay eggs and **rear** their **young** there.

Swallows feed insects to their hungry chicks.

In autumn swallows get ready to migrate. They fly south to spend the winter in South Africa where it is warmer.

*Large **flocks** gather together to fly off.*

Arctic terns

Arctic terns migrate further than any other animal. The birds **breed** in the Arctic during the summer months. They stay in the Arctic until the weather gets colder.

On their journey, Arctic terns feed in the air as they fly.

Arctic terns have to keep their chicks safe from harm.

In winter, Arctic terns fly south to Antarctica and Australia. After six months they fly half way round the world again, back to the Arctic to breed.

Migration map

Around the world, animals make different migration journeys at different times of the year. Do you recognise any of these animals and their journeys?

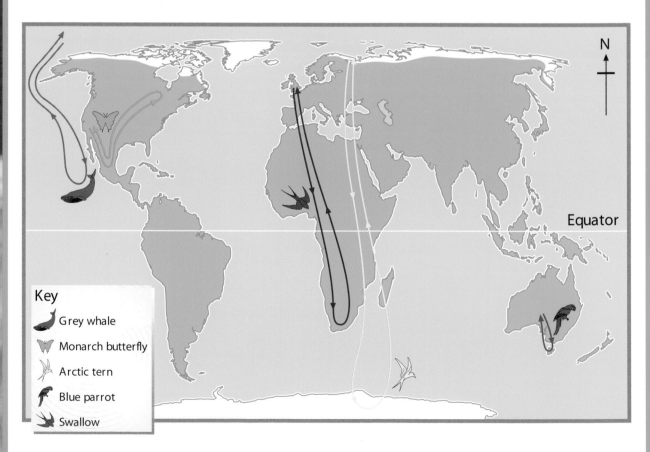

N

Equator

Key

Grey whale

Monarch butterfly

Arctic tern

Blue parrot

Swallow

Find out more about Nature's Patterns at www.heinemannexplore.co.uk

Glossary

blubber a layer of fat under the skin

breed have babies

flock group of birds

hatch break out of an egg

migrate move to a new place to live

pastures land covered with grass where animals eat

pattern something that happens over and over again

rear bring up young

season time of year. Each season has a special type of weather and temperature.

young baby form of an animal

More books to read

Animals in Danger: Blue Whale, Rod Theodorou (Heinemann Library, 2001)

Life Cycle of a Salmon, Angela Royston (Heinemann Library, 2000)

Nature's Patterns: Weather Patterns, Monica Hughes (Heinemann Library, 2004)

Index

autumn 8, 19, 20, 27

breeding 13, 14, 17, 18, 23, 25, 28, 29

feeding 8, 9, 10, 11

group migration 20, 21, 22, 23, 27

season 10, 26

spring 21, 23, 26

summer 25, 28

weather 8, 11, 21, 22, 27, 28

winter 9, 22, 24, 27

yearly migration 7, 8, 10, 16, 17, 22, 24, 26, 28

Titles in the *Nature's Patterns* series include:

Hardback   0 431 11397 1

Hardback   0 431 11396 3

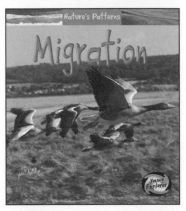

Hardback   0 431 11394 7

Hardback   0 431 11393 9

Hardback   0 431 11395 5

Find out about the other titles in this series on our website www.heinemann.co.uk/library